GALE
CENGAGE Learning

Novels for Students, Volume 14

Staff

Editor: Jennifer Smith.

Contributing Editors: Anne Marie Hacht, Michael L. LaBlanc, Ira Mark Milne, Daniel Toronto, Carol Ullmann.

Managing Editor, Content: Dwayne D. Hayes.

Managing Editor, Product: David Galens.

Publisher, Literature Product: Mark Scott.

Literature Content Capture: Joyce Nakamura, *Managing Editor*. Sara Constantakis, *Editor*.

Research: Victoria B. Cariappa, *Research Manager*. Sarah Genik, Ron Morelli, Tamara Nott, Tracie A. Richardson, *Research Associates*. Nicodemus Ford, *Research Assistant*.

Permissions: Maria L. Franklin, *Permissions Manager*. Shalice Shah-Caldwell, *Permissions*

Associate. Deborah Freitas, *IC Coordinator/Permissions Associate.*

Manufacturing: Mary Beth Trimper, *Manager, Composition and Electronic Prepress.* Evi Seoud, *Assistant Manager, Composition Purchasing and Electronic Prepress.* Stacy Melson, *Buyer.*

Imaging and Multimedia Content Team: Barbara Yarrow, *Manager.* Randy Bassett, *Imaging Supervisor.* Robert Duncan, Dan Newell, Luke Rademacher, *Imaging Specialists.* Pamela A. Reed, *Imaging Coordinator.* Leitha Etheridge-Sims, Mary Grimes, David G. Oblender, *Image Catalogers.* Robyn V. Young, *Project Manager.* Dean Dauphinais, *Senior Image Editor.* Kelly A. Quin, *Image Editor.*

Product Design Team: Pamela A. E. Galbreath, *Senior Art Director.* Michael Logusz, *Graphic Artist.*

Copyright Notice

agency, institution, publication, service, or individual does not imply endorsement of the editors or publisher. Errors brought to the attention of the publisher and verified to the satisfaction of the publisher will be corrected in future editions.

For Whom the Bell Tolls

Ernest Hemingway 1940

Introduction

When *For Whom the Bell Tolls* was published in 1940, it immediately became a resounding critical and popular success and helped cement Ernest Hemingway's reputation as one of America's foremost writers. Readers praised its realistic portrait of not only the political tensions in Europe that would soon erupt into World War II but also the complexities of the entire experience of war for the individual who found him or herself fighting for a cause. Hemingway had previously explored this theme, most notably in his short story collection, *In Our Time* (1924), and in his novels *The Sun Also Rises* (1926) and *A Farewell to Arms* (1929). Yet his attitude toward his subject in *For Whom the Bell Tolls* reveals a subtle shift. While his previous works focused more on the meaninglessness of war, this novel ends with a reaffirmation of community.

For Whom the Bell Tolls chronicles the experiences of American college professor Robert Jordan, who has volunteered to fight for the Loyalist cause in the Spanish Civil War. His initial idealism is quickly tempered by the realities of war. Yet his courage enables him to remain devoted to the cause, even as he faces death. Hemingway's compassionate and authentic portrait of his characters as they struggle to retain their idealistic beliefs has helped earn the novel its reputation as one of Hemingway's finest.

Author Biography

Ernest Hemingway was born on July 21, 1899, in Oak Park, Illinois, to Clarence Edmunds (physician) and Grace (music teacher) Hemingway, both strict Congregationalists. He started writing when he was a teenager, penning a weekly column for his high school newspaper. During this period, he also began to write poems and stories, some of which were published in his school's literary magazine. After graduating high school in 1917, Hemingway started his career as a reporter for the *Kansas City Star*, covering city crime and writing feature stories. The position helped him develop a journalistic style, which would later become one of the most identifiable characteristics of his fiction.

When World War I broke out, he volunteered as a Red Cross ambulance driver in Italy. After suffering severe leg injuries, Hemingway met and fell in love with a nurse who would eventually break off their relationship. Disillusioned with the war and with romantic relationships, Hemingway returned home and turned his attention to fiction writing. To support himself, however, he returned to reporting, accepting a position at the *Toronto Star*.

Like many of his compatriots of the Lost Generation, Hemingway left America for Europe, where he joined the group of literary expatriates in Paris, including Gertrude Stein and F. Scott Fitzgerald. He lived in Paris for the next seven years, working on his fiction and serving as a European correspondent for American newspapers. From 1937 to 1938, he covered the Spanish Civil War, and from 1944 to 1945, he reported on the battles of World War II.

Edward J. O'Brien named Hemingway's short story "My Old Man," which appeared in his first publication, *Three Stories and Ten Poems*, in his list of the best stories of 1923. Hemingway's next publication, a series of short stories interspersed with vignettes, entitled *In Our Time* (1924), was well received, and he began to earn a reputation as an astute chronicler of the Lost Generation. This reputation was solidified after the publication of his next story collection, *Men Without Women* (1927), and the novels *The Sun Also Rises* (1926) and *A Farewell to Arms* (1929). When *For Whom the Bell Tolls* was published in 1940, it was regarded by the public and the critics as one of his best works.

Along with his growing reputation as one of the most important contemporary American writers, Hemingway developed a mythic persona that he helped perpetuate. During the middle of the century, the public began to envision Hemingway as the personification of his heroes—a hard drinking, forceful American, who could stand his ground on the battlefield, in the boxing ring, and on safari. Several American magazines, such as *Life* and *Esquire*, chronicled his adventures. Yet, during this period, he also devoted himself to his craft, which he considered of paramount importance in his life and his time.

During the 1950s, a life of alcohol abuse and rough living took a toll on his health. His health problems, compounded by his three failed marriages and periods of creative stagnation, resulted in a mental breakdown in 1960, and the following year on July 2, Hemingway committed suicide in Ketchum, Idaho.

Hemingway has retained his reputation as one of America's most significant and influential writers. During his long literary career, he earned several accolades, including the Pulitzer Prize in 1953 for *The Old Man and the Sea*, the Nobel Prize for literature in 1954, and the Award of Merit from the American Academy of Arts & Letters in 1954.

Plot Summary

The novel chronicles the experiences of American professor Robert Jordan from Saturday afternoon to Tuesday noon during the last week of May 1937. Jordan has volunteered to fight with the Loyalist guerrilla army in the Spanish Civil War. His mission is to blow up a bridge near Segovia prior to a Loyalist offensive in that area, scheduled to occur in three days. When the novel opens, he is behind enemy lines, ready to meet up with Pablo and his wife Pilar, his contacts, and the leaders of one of the guerrilla factions.

Jordan studies the bridge as he determines how he will blow it up at the necessary moment. He has previously blown up bridges and trains, but he never has had to time a demolition so carefully. Pablo and Pilar have been set to help Jordan plan and execute the mission, gathering together other guerrilla bands if necessary.

Jordan finds Pablo and Pilar and travels with them to their hideout in a mountain cave where he meets Maria, a beautiful young woman. Maria has escaped the Fascists after being tortured and raped. Jordan also meets Anselmo at the hideout, an elderly guerrilla fighter who is determined to die, if need be, for the Loyalist cause. Even though he recognizes that the Loyalists have committed atrocities during the war, Jordan has aligned himself with them, blaming their poverty and oppression for their cruel actions. He hates the Fascists as much as the others do, noting that their cruelty stems not from a desire for freedom but from naked ambition and a lust for power. After hearing Maria's shocking tales of abuse, Jordan redoubles his determination to kill as many Fascists as he can, even if he sacrifices his own life as a result.

That evening, however, he begins to fall in love with Maria, after spending most of the night with her, and considers a future with her. As a result, for the first time, Jordan becomes fearful about the mission since he now has something to live for other than stopping the Fascist occupation. He knows, though, that fear will prevent him from keeping a cool head as he plans his operation.

Jordan is able to suppress his fears, and he carefully plans the destruction of the bridge, drawing several sketches to familiarize himself and the other guerrillas with the area and to determine the best course of action. The operation, however, is almost destroyed by Pablo, who, fearing for his safety, deserts the camp after stealing the explosives.

Pablo returns on the third morning after having a change of heart, accompanied by more Loyalists with horses. The explosives and detonators, however, have been damaged so severely that Jordan has no other choice than to try to blow up the bridge with hand grenades, which would be a much more dangerous task.

The group begins to carry out their mission,

unaware that the anticipated Loyalist advance has failed. First, Jordan and Anselmo kill the guards while Pablo and the others attack the Fascists who are approaching the bridge, in order to slow their movement. After Jordan blows up the bridge, he scrambles to safety. Anselmo, however, has been hit by falling debris and dies. Jordan blames Pablo for the death of the old man, determining that if they had used the explosives, they all would have been safe.

Jordan reunites with Pablo, Pilar, Maria, and two of the men Pablo had brought with him. Pablo insists that the others had been killed in the battle, but Jordan determines that Pablo had killed them for their horses. Pablo acknowledges the murders with a shrug, noting that the men had not been part of his group.

Jordan plans their escape away from the front. He insists that Pablo should go first, since he knows the territory, accompanied by Maria. Jordan knows that those in front will have the best chance of reaching safety before the Fascists discover them. He then sends Pilar and the two guerillas on and follows them. The others make it safely across the open road, but Jordan is injured when his horse, wounded by the Fascists' bullets, falls on him. The others pull him out of the line of fire, but he insists that they go on ahead and leave him there, knowing that his injuries would slow them down and place them all in danger. Despondent, Maria tries to convince him to allow her to stay with him, but he refuses, insisting that he will live through her. The others have to carry her away.

After the others leave, Jordan sits against a tree with his gun propped up in his lap and waits for the Fascists, hoping to slow them down as the others escape. As he waits, he thinks about what has brought him to this point and determines that he has done the best that he could and thus his death will not be in vain. The novel ends as Jordan sees a Fascist lieutenant coming into view and prepares to fire.

Characters

Anselmo

Anselmo is an elderly member of Pablo's band. Anselmo lacks education but reveals a moral and compassionate nature. He supplies the human element to the struggle that Jordan and Pablo so often ignore, as he embodies the Loyalist ideals to which the two men had originally devoted their lives. Each time he witnesses or participates in a killing, the event profoundly troubles him. He is killed as he helps Jordan blow up the bridge.

General Golz

General Golz is one of the Russians who have been sent to help the Loyalist army. He oversees the upcoming planned attack against the Fascists.

Media Adaptations

- *For Whom the Bell Tolls* was adapted as a film by Sam Wood, with a screenplay by Dudley Nichols, starring Gary Cooper and Ingrid Bergman, from Paramount, 1943. It is available on video and DVD.

- An audio version, read by Alexander Adams, has been published by Books on Tape.

Robert Jordan

Before the Spanish Civil War, Robert Jordan had been a college Spanish instructor with a deep love of Spain and its people. His liberal political leanings prompted him to join the Loyalists in their fight against the Fascists. Initially, he idealized the Loyalist cause and the character of its devotees, but as the novel begins, with Jordan embroiled in the realities of war, he experiences a profound disillusionment. He notes that his devotion to the cause had been almost like a religious experience, likening it to "the feeling you expected to have but did not have when you made your first communion." That "purity of feeling," however, soon dissipated. He has observed atrocities on both sides of the con-flict and has been chided for his naivete and "slight political development." At Gaylord's Hotel in Madrid, where he heard the callousness of the Russian officers, he concluded that they could "corrupt very easily" but then wondered "was it corruption or was it merely that you lost the naivete that you started with?"

He has come to the realization that most of the people of Spain have, like him, become disillusioned about their noble cause and so are not as willing to sacrifice themselves to it. As a result, he no longer defines himself as a communist; now he insists instead that he is an "anti-fascist," not a firm supporter of a cause but at least a dissenter to a movement he finds abhorrent.

His sense of duty compels him to complete the task he has taken on—the blowing up of a bridge in Fascist territory in an effort to aid the Loyalists' advance—even when he understands the probability of failure and the danger to himself and others. His courage, evident throughout the novel as he carries out his perilous mission, faces its greatest test after the mission fails to impede the Fascist movements and he suffers a severe injury when his horse stumbles. Understanding that his injuries will slow the others' escape, he convinces them to go on ahead to safety without him. He quickly overcomes his desire to kill himself and determines to face the oncoming Fascist forces in a last effort to help his comrades escape.

Maria

Jordan meets the young and beautiful Maria at Pablo's hideout. She has been brutalized by the Fascists after they murdered her father, a Loyalist mayor. Fascist sympathizers shaved her head as punishment for her association with the enemy, and, as a result, she is tagged with the nickname "Rabbit," which also suggests her timid demeanor. She gains strength, however, through her intense and short-lived love affair with Jordan.

Several critics, including Leslie Fiedler, have noted that Maria, like many of Hemingway's women, lacks development. She appears in the novel as an idealized image of a devoted woman who enjoys extreme sexual pleasure in her relationship with the protagonist. She seems to exist in the novel as tool to help reveal Jordan's character and to provide him with a sense of meaning. By the end of the novel, he must decide between his love for her and his duty to his compatriots.

Maria's immediate sexual attraction to Jordan seems unlikely given the sexual abuse she has repeatedly experienced at the hands of the Fascists. Yet her romantic insistence on staying with the injured Jordan at the end of the novel inspires readers' sympathy.

Pablo

Pablo serves as a foil to Jordan. He is the leader of the central guerrilla band and Pilar's husband. Prior to Jordan's appearance, he had earned the group's fearful respect. Yet, when Jordan challenges his authority and outlines the dangerous plan to blow up the bridge, Pablo's cowardice and self-absorption emerge. He tries to cover his fear by insisting that the mission is too dangerous, claiming that the lives of his men would be put at risk and their headquarters would most likely be discovered, since it is close to the bridge. His men, however, determine that they will follow Jordan's plan of action in an effort to ensure a Loyalist victory.

Pablo's vicious battle with Jordan for supremacy over the group, coupled with the fear that he will endanger the mission, prompts the band to consider killing him, but Pablo escapes with the explosives before they can act. Pablo's return to the group the next morning appears to be generated by his feelings of remorse over his actions; yet his primary motive may be his jealously over Maria's love for Jordan. When he returns, he insists that he now wholeheartedly supports the mission.

Hemingway suggests that, like Jordan, Pablo has lost his idealism by witnessing the brutalities of war on both sides. His acknowledgment of these atrocities has weakened his resolve to fight for the cause and has made him fearful for his own safety. Yet, though Jordan also at some points in the story becomes afraid for his life, he eventually exhibits the strength of character necessary to help ensure the safety of the others in the group. Pablo too often gives in to fears for his own safety and to jealousy over Jordan's power and his relationship with Maria.

Yet his character is contradictory. When Pilar asks him why he did not kill Jordan when he had the opportunity, Pablo replies that Jordan is "a good boy." Pablo appears to redeem himself at the end of the novel when he admits that he returned to the camp because, as he describes his desertion, "having done such a thing, there is a loneliness that cannot be borne." Ironically, Jordan must depend on Pablo for the group's survival. After Jordan is severely wounded, Pablo leads the rest of them to safety.

Pliar

Pilar is married to Pablo, the leader of the central guerrilla band. Unlike many of Hemingway's other women, Pilar is a complex, strong woman who does not allow her husband to dominate her. When Pablo's actions threaten to subvert their mission, Pilar promptly takes over as leader of the guerrillas. Hemingway suggests that Jordan could not have carried out his mission without her. She comes to represent in the novel the ideals and dedication of the Spanish Loyalists.

She also helps engineer Jordan and Maria's relationship, giving her as a gift to him. Pilar tells Maria that she supports and encourages her union with Jordan but admits that their relationship will make her jealous. Pilar insists that she is "no *tortillera* (lesbian) but a woman made for men": "I do not make perversions," she claims, yet she refuses to explain her jealousy.

Michael Reynolds, in his article "Ringing the Changes: Hemingway's 'Bell' Tolls Fifty," writes that this scene, more than any other, reveals her complexity. Hemingway, he notes, "who would become increasingly fascinated with such triangles, realized the androgynous side of men and women earlier than most have given him credit." Pilar has insisted elsewhere, "I would have made a good man, but I am all woman and ugly. Yet many men have loved me and I have loved many men." However, as Reynolds notes, Hemingway has characterized her as androgynous, juxtaposing her insistence of her attraction to men with her tenderly holding Maria at the end of the novel, as the band leaves Jordan behind, waiting to die.

Her strength of character also emerges in her supernatural powers. When she reads Jordan's palm, she foresees his death, yet she stays devoted to the mission even at the risk of her own life. Her powers of perception allow her to recognize the depths of Jordan's and Maria's suffering, which prompts her to help them come together.

Pilar serves as the group's storyteller, spinning her stories as appropriate thematic backdrops to the action. As the group prepares for their mission, she tells the story of Finito, a bullfighter overcome by fear in the bullring, and of Pablo and his men murdering Fascist sympathizers by throwing them over a cliff.

El Sordo

El Sordo is the leader of a neighboring guerrilla band. Jordan asks him and his men to join

Pablo's band to help blow up the bridge.

Idealism

The elderly peasant Anselmo most fully represents the Loyalist ideals in the novel. Hemingway suggests that his lack of education and his compassionate nature allow him to believe in the cause and to fight for it to the end of his life. Through his idealism, he supplies the human element to the struggle that Jordan and Pablo so often ignore.

Pablo has largely forgotten the ideals of the cause to which he had originally devoted his life. He has seen too much of the reality of war and so participates now more out of self-interest than out of patriotism. As a result, he can take pleasure in his brutal murder of the Fascists. And when he considers the plan to blow up the bridge too dangerous, he flees with the explosives. Yet he appears to retain some of the ideals to which he once dedicated himself. When Pilar asks him why he did not kill Jordan when he had the opportunity, Pablo replies that Jordan is "a good boy," since his motives are noble. He also notes the camaraderie that results from devotion to the cause when, as he describes his desertion, he notes, "having done such a thing, there is a loneliness that cannot be borne."

Jordan struggles to retain his sense of idealism throughout the novel. Initially, he volunteers to serve with the Loyalists because of his liberal attitudes toward politics and his deep love of the Spanish people. However, he quickly gets a taste of the reality of war when he sees atrocities committed on both sides. He notes that his education on the true politics of war came as he listened to the cynical attitude of the Russian officers at Gaylord's in Madrid as they discussed their intentions to pervert the Loyalists' devotion to their cause for their own ends. This attitude is reflected in the opening chapter as Jordan discusses the mission with Golz, who focuses only on the military aspect of the plan.

Courage

Jordan's courage emerges in the face of his growing disillusionment. James Nagel, in his article on Hemingway for the *Dictionary of Literary Biography*, notes that Jordan "has a realistic skepticism about what the war will actually accomplish, but he dedicates himself fully to the cause nonetheless." Even though he suspects the mission will fail, he carefully plans and executes it, accepting the fact that failure most likely will result in death. His relationship with Maria helps provide him with the strength to continue as he allows himself to envision a future with her. His final act of courage appears at the end of the novel, as he faces imminent death at the hands of the Fascists. His fear initially prompts him to consider suicide. However, his strength of character returns when he recognizes that he can help ensure the safety of the rest of the group by staying alive to delay the advance of the Fascists.

Style

Point of View

The novel presents the narrative through an omniscient point of view that continually shifts back and forth between the characters. In this way, Hemingway can effectively chronicle the effect of the war on the men and women involved. The narrator shifts from Anselmo's struggles in the snow during his watch to Pilar's story about Pablo's execution of Fascists and El Sordo's lonely death to help readers more clearly visualize their experiences.

In "Ringing the Changes: Hemingway's 'Bell' Tolls Fifty," Michael Reynolds writes, "Without drawing undue attention to his artistry, Hemingway has written a collection of short stories embedded in a framing novel." Against the backdrop of the group's attempt to blow up the bridge, each character tells his or her own story: Maria tells of her parents' murder and her rape; Jordan shares what he learned about the true politics of war at Gaylord's in Madrid. Pilar provides the most compelling and comprehensive stories of Finito's fears in the bullfighting ring and of Pablo and his men as they beat the Fascists to death in a drunken rage.

Hemingway employs flashbacks and flashforwards to enhance thematic focus. Pilar's stories of struggle and heroism make their mission all the more poignant and place it in an historical context. Jordan's flashbacks to a time when his ideals were not tempered by the reality of war highlight his growing sense of disillusionment. His dreams of a future with Maria in Madrid add a bittersweet touch to his present predicament and his final death scene.

Style

One of Hemingway's most distinct and celebrated characteristics is his deliberate writing style. Trained as a newspaper reporter, Hemingway used a journalistic style in his fiction, honed down to economical, abrupt descriptions of characters and events. His goal was to ensure that his words accurately described reality. The best example of his economical style comes at the end of the novel, as Jordan faces death. Hemingway's spare, direct description of Jordan's final moments as he considers suicide and then determines to survive long enough to help the group escape reflects Jordan's stoicism and his acceptance of the inevitable.

Topics for Further Study

- Watch the film version of *For Whom the Bell Tolls*. Do you think the film is dated? What scenes would you update for today's audience?

- Compare the portrait of war in *A Farewell to Arms* to that of *For Whom the Bell Tolls*. How are they simliar? What differences do you see? Which resonates the most for you as the reader, and why?

- Research the Loyalist sympathizers during the Spanish Civil War. Do Hemingway's guerrilla bands in *For Whom the Bell Tolls* represent an accurate portrayal of the Loyalist faction during this war? Explain your answer.

- Some critics find the relationship

between Jordan and Maria to be overly romantic and unrealistic. Support or refute this conclusion.

The Spanish Civil War

Civil war broke out in Spain in 1936, but the underlying causes can be traced back several years prior to that date. In the 1930s Spain experienced continuous political upheavals. In 1931, after years of civil conflict in the country, King Alfonso XIII voluntarily placed himself in exile, and on April 13 of that year, a new republic emerged. The Leftist government, however, faced similar civil unrest, and by 1933, the conservatives regained control. By 1936 the people voted the leftists back in. After the assassination of Jose Calvas Otelo, an influential Monarchist, the army led a revolt against the government and sponsored the return of General Francisco Franco, who had been exiled because of his politics.

As a result, civil war broke out across the country between the Loyalist-leftists and the Monarchist-rightists. Russia backed the leftists while Germany and Italy supported the rightists. The war continued until 1939 with each side committing atrocities: the leftists slaughtered religious and political figures while the rightists bombed civilian targets. At the beginning of 1936, the Loyalists were suffering from an effective blockade as Franco's troops gained control. On March 28, the war ended as the rightists took the city of Madrid.

Hemingway, siding with the Loyalists, first lent his support to their cause by raising money for ambulances and medical supplies. In 1937, he ran the Ambulances Committee of the American Friends of Spanish Democracy. During the war, he often returned to Spain as a journalist, penning articles for the *North American Newspaper Alliance* and *Esquire*. When the Fascist army won control of Spain in 1939, Hemingway had just started writing *For Whom the Bell Tolls*.

Compare & Contrast

- **1930s–1940s:** The world experiences a decade of aggression in the 1930s that culminates in World War II. This second world war results from the rise of totalitarian regimes in Germany, Italy, and Japan. One week after Nazi Germany and the USSR sign the Treaty of Nonaggression, Germany invades Poland, and World War II begins.

  Today: The world is threatened by Islamic fundamentalist groups who have declared a holy war against the West. These radical groups have committed terrorist acts in several countries including the United States. On September 11, 2001, the most devastating acts of terror to date worldwide are delivered as terrorists fly planes into the World Trade Center Towers in New York City and into the Pentagon and are responsible for the crash of another plane in Pennsylvania.

- **1930s–1940s:** Civil war breaks out in Spain in 1936 between the Fascists, backed by Germany and Italy, and the Loyalists, backed by the USSR.

  Today: Spain has been established as a social and democratic country that is governed by a parliamentary monarchy. National sovereignty is vested in the Spanish people.

- **1930s–1940s:** American women gain a measure of independence in the workplace as they labor in the factories, replacing men who have gone to war. By 1945, the peak of the war production, approximately 19 million women hold jobs. Independence is difficult to relinquish when, at the end of the war, the men come home and demand their jobs back, and their wives return to their traditional roles in the home.

  Today: American women have made major gains in their fight for equality even without the 1972 Equal Rights Amendment Bill. Discrimination against women is now against the law.

The Lost Generation

This term became associated with a group of American writers in the 1920s who felt a growing sense of disillusionment after World War I. As a result, many left America for Europe. T. S. Eliot and Ezra Pound initially relocated to London, while F. Scott Fitzgerald and Hemingway traveled to Paris, which appeared to offer them a much freer society than America or England did. During this period, Paris became a mecca for these expatriates, who congregated in literary salons, restaurants, and bars to discuss their work in the context of the new age. One such salon was dominated by Gertrude Stein, who at one gathering insisted "you are all a lost generation," a quote immortalized by Hemingway in the preface to *The Sun Also Rises*. That novel, like *For Whom the Bell Tolls* and Fitzgerald's *The Great Gatsby*, presents a penetrating portrait of this Lost Generation.

The characters in works by these authors reflected the authors' growing sense of disillusionment along with the new ideas in psychology, anthropology, and philosophy that had become popular in the early part of the century. Freudianism, for example, which had caused a loosening of sexual morality during the Jazz Age, began to be studied by these writers as they explored the psyches of their characters and recorded their often subjective points of view of themselves and their world. Hemingway's men and women faced a meaningless world with courage and dignity, exhibiting "grace under pressure," while Fitzgerald's sought the redemptive power of love in a world driven by materialism.

This age of confusion, redefinition, and experimentation produced one of the most fruitful periods in American letters. These writers helped create a new form of literature, later called modernism, which repudiated traditional literary conventions. Prior to the twentieth century, writers structured their works to reflect their belief in the stability of character and the intelligibility of experience. Traditionally, novels and stories ended with a clear sense of closure, as conflicts were resolved and characters gained knowledge about themselves and their world. The authors of the Lost Generation challenged these assumptions as they expanded the genre's traditional form to accommodate their characters' questions about the individual's place in the world.

Critical Overview

When *For Whom the Bell Tolls* was published in 1940, Hemingway's reputation as one of America's most important writers was already well established. The new novel received overwhelmingly positive reviews from critics and the public alike, with many insisting that it was Hemingway's best novel to date. It quickly became a bestseller, as the first printing's 210,000 copies immediately sold out. In less than six months, that figure jumped to over 491,000. Michael Reynolds, in his assessment of the novel for the *Virginia Quarterly Review*, notes that a reviewer in the *New York Times* insisted that it was "the best book Ernest Hemingway has written, the fullest, the deepest, the truest. It will be one of the major novels in American literature." Reynolds adds that Dorothy Parker claimed that it was "beyond all comparison, Ernest Hemingway's finest book," and an article in the *Nation* proclaimed that it set "a new standard for Hemingway in characterization, dialogue, suspense and compassion."

These and other critics praised Hemingway's thematic focus on idealism and responsibility, especially as a reflection of the mood of the times, as the world braced for the devastation of the impending world war. Reynolds writes, though, that the novel "transcends the historical context that bore it, becoming a parable rather than a paradigm."

Later, however, some critics found fault with the novel's politics. Hemingway's inclusion of Loyalist as well as Fascist atrocities drew criticism from liberal sympathizers. Other critics have complained about the idealized relationship between Jordan and Maria. Leslie A. Fiedler, for example, in his *Love and Death in the American Novel*, finds fault in all of Hemingway's characterizations of love. He comments that if, in *For Whom the Bell Tolls*, Hemingway "has written the most absurd love scene in the history of the American novel, this is not because he lost momentarily his skill and authority." Fiedler suggests that the love affair between Jordan and Maria "illuminates the whole erotic content of his fiction."

While the novel has never regained the critical status it enjoyed when it was first published, the novel is currently regarded, as James Nagel notes in his article on Hemingway for *Dictionary of Literary Biography*, as "nearly perfect." Philip Young in *American Writers* comments, "none of his books had evoked more richly the life of the senses, had shown a surer sense of plotting, or provided more fully living secondary characters, or livelier dialogue." Reynolds concludes his review with the following assessment: "And thus, softly, across time, *For Whom the Bell Tolls* continues in muted tones to toll for us."

Sources

Fiedler, Leslie A., *Love and Death in the American Novel*, Dell, 1960.

Nagel, James, "Ernest Hemingway," in *Dictionary of Literary Biography*, Volume 9: *American Novelists, 1910–1945*, Gale Research, 1981, pp. 100-20.

Reynolds, Michael, "Ringing the Changes: Hemingway's *Bell* Tolls Fifty," in *Virginia Quarterly Review*, Vol. 67, No. 1, Winter 1991, pp. 1-18.

Young, Philip, "Ernest Hemingway," in *American Writers*, Vol. 2, 1974, pp. 247-70.

Further Reading

Buckley, Ramon, "Revolution in Ronda: The Facts in Hemingway's *For Whom the Bell Tolls*," in *Hemingway Review*, Vol. 17, No 1, Fall 1997, pp. 49-57.

> Buckley places the novel in its historical context.

Martin, Robert A., "Robert Jordan and the Spanish Country: Learning to Live in It 'Truly and Well,'" in *Hemingway Review*, Vol. 16, No. 1, Fall 1996, pp. 56-64.

> Martin presents a close analysis of the character of Robert Jordan and his relationship to Spanish culture.

Meyers, Jeffrey, "*For Whom the Bell Tolls* as Contemporary History," in *The Spanish Civil War in Literature*, edited by Janet Perez and Wendell Aycock, Texas Tech University Press, 1990, pp. 85-107.

> This essay explores the political implications of the novel.

Wylder, Delbert E., "*For Whom the Bell Tolls:* The Mythic Hero in the Contemporary World," in *Hemingway's Heroes*, University of New Mexico Press, 1969, pp. 127-64.

> Wylder presents an analysis of Robert Jordan who, he writes,

"follows the mythical journey of the hero in a modern setting."

CPSIA information can be obtained
at www.ICGtesting.com
Printed in the USA
LVOW13s1746311017
554455LV00010B/631/P